THE WALNUT DIET AND FITNESS PLAN

DR FRANK RYAN

SWIFT PUBLISHERS LTD

Swift Publishers Ltd
Refuge Assurance House, Market Street, Bromsgrove,
Worcestershire, B61 8DA, England.

Swift Publishers Ltd, England
A subsidiary of Swift Consolidated Holdings PLC

British Library Cataloguing-in-Publication Data

Ryan, Dr Frank
The Walnut Diet and Fitness Plan
I. World – Medical Self Help
II. Title
ISBN 1 874082 16 2

First published in Great Britain by Swift Publishers 1993

Designed & typeset in Columbus by Armitage Typo/Graphics
Riverside Studios, Dogley Mill, Fenay Bridge, Huddersfield HD8 OLE

Printed and bound in the UK by Harper Collins, Wester Hill Road, Bishopbriggs, Glasgow G20

Acknowledgements

I would like to thank Professor Gary E Fraser and Professor Joan Sabaté of the Loma Linda University, for their help with information on the Adventist studies.

Contents

Chapter One
What's special about walnuts?
page 7

Chapter Two
A healthy lifestyle should also be fun
page 17

Chapter Three
Delicious walnut recipes
page 22

Chapter Four
Putting the Walnut Diet into practice
page 42

Chapter Five
The exercise plan
page 46

Chapter Six
Lifestyles
page 60

CHAPTER ONE

What's special about walnuts?

Heart attacks kill one in three men in our society and almost one in four women, making this the most serious medical problem we face today. A vast medical industry is devoted to this, often involving powerful drugs and surgery. I have prescribed many such medications myself over 23 years of hospital practice, during which the commonest medical emergency I have had to deal with has been heart attacks. Those long years, helping many thousands of heart attack victims, convinced me that it is far better to prevent heart attacks than to treat their consequences. It was equally obvious that preventive measures, if they were to be palatable and absolutely safe, should focus on a natural and wholesome approach.

While other life-style factors, in particular smoking, play an important part, there is abundant medical evidence that our Western diet, with its associated high blood cholesterol levels, is one of the most important causes of the heart attack epidemic we are facing today.

This is why I was very interested in a study by Loma Linda University, which suggested that by incorporating California walnuts into our diet we could dramatically reduce the blood cholesterol levels, thereby reducing the risk of a heart attack. It was the combination of this natural and wholesome message with its potential benefits to ordinary people that caused me to write this book.

An interesting group of people

The Seventh Day Adventists are a major Christian denomination whose careful lifestyles make them a useful population to study for heart disease. There are many known risk factors for heart attacks, including smoking, excessive alcohol consumption and excess saturated fat in the diet. This makes it rather difficult to disentangle the contribution of these different factors to the cause of heart attacks when studies are done on human populations. The fact that Adventists avoid smoking and excessive alcohol consumption makes it much easier to measure the effect of diet on their risk of death from heart attack.

There is a second reason why Adventists have become a very popular group of people to study for dietary health risks. Because of their concern with the poor health of ordinary Americans in the nineteenth century, the California Adventists founded their own medical institutions throughout the world. In the attractive southern Californian city of Loma Linda – in Spanish this means "Beautiful Hill" – the Adventists built a sanatorium which evolved into a Loma Linda University and Medical school, which is renowned throughout the world for its excellent services for the sick. What was more natural than for this first-class medical centre, built from the caring attitude and enterprise of American Adventists, to study risk factors for mortality on volunteers from the Adventists themselves.

The Loma Linda studies

Medical experts around the world became particularly interested when, in the mid 1960s, a major study was conducted by the Loma Linda University in California to examine the cause of death in 25,000 Adventists over a five-year period. What was even more interesting was that at the same time the American

Cancer Society was performing a very similar mortality study in non-Adventists in America.

Although these studies were first set up to study cancer deaths, they were quickly extended to include deaths from heart attacks and coronary artery disease. The results were striking.

Adventist women lived on average five to eight years longer than non-Adventist women and Adventist men lived two to five years longer than their non-Adventist counterparts.

The question was: Why?

Examination of the habits of the two test populations suggested that the longer survival and better health of the Adventists were due to the lower cigarette consumption, better diet, better exercise and less obesity. But like the best of scientific studies, it asked more questions than it answered. Soon a more searching study was begun which looked not at the difference between Adventists and other Americans but between different groups of Adventists themselves. The results of this study were even more interesting.

The Loma Linda heart attack study

Since it was easy to exclude the effects of smoking and alcohol, because these groups did not smoke or drink, the next study, which began in 1974 and included almost 35,000 people, could look to the effects of diet alone on mortality patterns. This study, which was one of the biggest of its kind in the world, showed that people's diets could dramatically affect their risks of dying at a younger age. People who ate higher quantities of red meat, fatty foods, eggs and coffee had a much greater risk of early death than people who made a point of including fruit and vegetables in their diet. When they looked at deaths in people between the ages of 30 and 50, those people who ate a lot of fat from meat had an astonishing four times the risk of death. This increased risk continued even up to the age of 80. This study suggested that people with the best chance of living longer were thin non-smokers, given to regular exercise and with a diet high in fruit and vegetables.

Perhaps one of the most surprising findings of this research – and a finding very relevant to the new information on the health-giving properties of walnuts – was the fact that people who ate nuts at least four times a week incurred only half the risk of death from a heart attack as people who did not regularly eat nuts. Of sixty-five foods which were analysed for effect, nuts seemed to give the most consistent and protective effect against heart attacks.

This finding was so striking it soon became the subject of further study to discover why nuts should have such health-giving properties.

Blood cholesterol and the risk of heart attacks

We are all aware that people with a raised blood cholesterol level, especially a type of cholesterol called LDL-cholesterol, are at an increased risk of dying from a heart attack. There is a good explanation for this. When the blood cholesterol level is high, it tends to be deposited on the inner lining of our arteries, as shown in the following diagram.

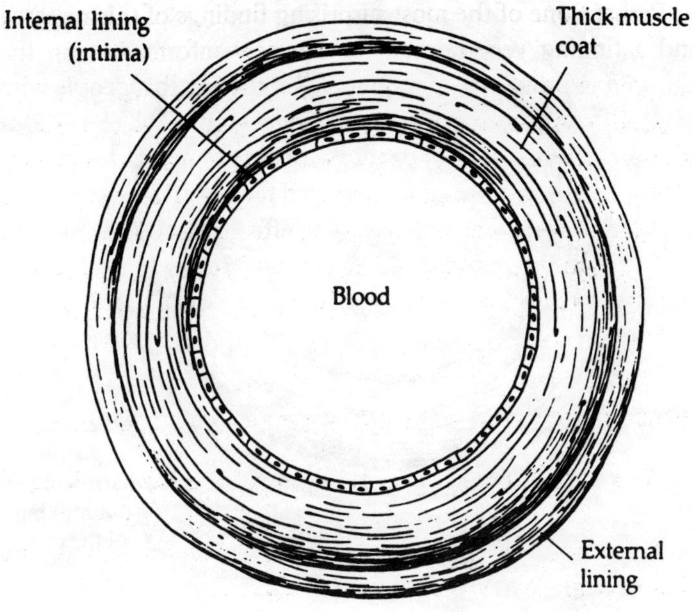

This thickening on the lining of the artery is called an atheromatous plaque. If the narrowing involves an artery to the heart muscle, called a coronary artery, it tends to cause chest pain on exertion, particularly walking, which is called angina. Even more importantly, the narrowed segment of the coronary artery is liable to clot, causing a complete blockage to the blood flow through it. This is the usual mechanism of a heart attack.

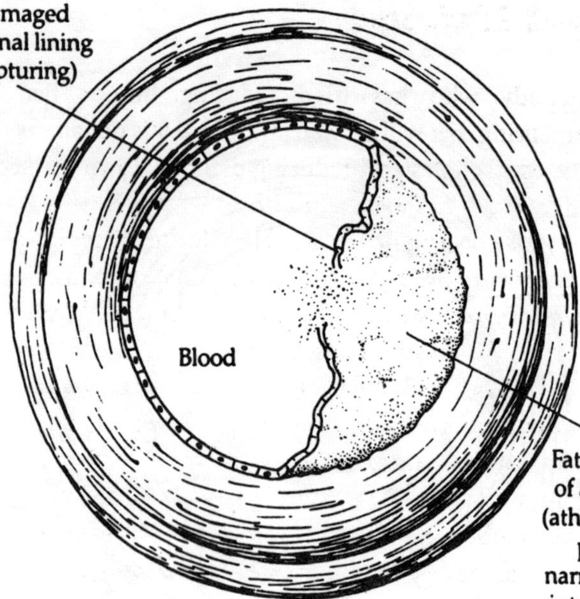

Any treatment that helps to lower the blood level of cholesterol is likely to reduce the risk of atheroma and heart attacks. The research workers at Loma Linda University were well aware that California Walnuts, grown locally, were a dietary favourite with many of the people taking part in the Adventist Study. The important question was now obvious: why did those people who ate California Walnuts regularly have only half the risk of dying from a heart attack? Did eating walnuts regularly reduce the high-risk LDL blood cholesterol, leading to the dramatic reduction in heart attack risk?

The team of research workers at Loma Linda University now set out to test this hypothesis.

California Walnuts and blood cholesterol – the Loma Linda study

Anybody who has tried reducing his or her blood cholesterol using diet will be well aware that it is not an easy thing to do. The usual cholesterol-reducing diet cuts down markedly on saturated fats such as those found in red meat and dairy produce, including full-cream milk, cream and cheeses. People find this hard because they often like to eat these kinds of foods. There are several other reasons why low fat diets are difficult. When you eat fat it quickly satisfies your hunger feelings so you tend to feel full and content for many hours afterwards. Other ingredients in your diet do not give you quite the same feeling of fullness and satisfaction. To make matters even more difficult, people on very low fat diets may run into difficulties with having too few fat soluble vitamins, such as D and A, minerals such as calcium and other essential dietary ingredients called "essential fatty acids", because these are normally only found within the fat in your diet.

Walnuts contain vegetable oils, which are another form of fat. Almost all of the fat in walnuts is polyunsaturated – the ratio of polyunsaturated to saturated fat in walnuts is 7 to 1, which is one of the highest found in natural foods. As many of my readers will already know, polyunsaturated fat has long been shown to "protect" the heart by reducing blood cholesterol when compared to saturated fat, which has been shown to be a "risk" type of fat which raises the blood cholesterol. If it could be shown that replacing some of the saturated fats, which are mainly derived from red meat and dairy produce, with the largely polyunsatured fats found in walnuts, this might cause a beneficial lowering of the blood cholesterol. What was more, people replacing high fat foods such as red meats with walnuts would feel full and contented because, as most people will have discovered already, the oils in walnuts make them a very pleasant and satisfying food. Walnuts also provide many essential fats and vitamins.

This was the reason why the Loma Linda University investigators planned another scientific study to test the effects of walnuts on blood cholesterol.

Over a period of 61 days, they studied 18 healthy male volunteers, aged between 21 and 43 years. Their blood cholesterols were "normal" for their age group. The men came to a special scientific kitchen twice a day, seven days a week, where their food was prepared for them and where they ate breakfast and dinner. For their noon meal, they were given a prepared lunch to take away.

As you may know, it is not scientifically accurate enough just to go out and test people in this way. It is also necessary to compare the results of the test group with the results of a "control" group of people, who are put through an identical routine but without the walnuts in their diet. In this study, the research team used the same 18 men for both the test and control parts of the study, by testing half of them on either diet and then crossing them over to the other diet, so that each participant tried both the walnut diet and the control diet. To make sure there was no bias in the results, the doctors performing the test were not aware which diet the subjects were taking when they measured the cholesterol levels. To be even more exacting, the researchers took an additional precaution that really did test the ability of walnuts to reduce blood cholesterol in the most difficult of dietary conditions.

The control diet was not a normal diet at all but a standard diet used to lower blood cholesterol in people known to have raised blood levels, called the "National Cholesterol Education Program Diet". Essentially this cuts down the consumption of fat to 30% of total calories, with a third of these coming from saturated fat, and it is used as the conventional diet of the American Heart Association. Any nutritionist or dietitian will know how difficult it is to further lower cholesterol when somebody is already taking a cholesterol-lowering diet of this nature. The researchers tested the ability of walnuts to achieve exactly that.

On the walnut diet, the volunteers kept to the same cholesterol-lowering diet, but with smaller portions of meat, fish and poultry so that calories derived from these were replaced with the exact calorie equivalent of three ounces of walnuts each day.

The results were very interesting and of sufficient importance to be reported by Professor Sabat, Professor Fraser and colleagues in the March edition of the highly respectable medical journal, the *New England Journal of Medicine.*

> *"Even in these very exacting test conditions, the addition of walnuts to a diet that was already a standard cholesterol-lowering diet, lowered the blood LDL cholesterol by a further 16 percent and the mean blood cholesterol by 12.4 percent. This was considered a highly significant effect."*

Suddenly people became interested. Not only did they want to know how they might benefit from the health-giving properties of the walnut but they also wanted to know a little more of the history of a nut that had so long been familiar and yet about which they knew very little.

The California Walnut story

The walnut is one of the oldest tree foods and has been a wholesome natural food enjoyed by people since history began. There are two main types, the black walnut, native to America, and the commoner walnut we now call the "English" walnut, which in fact originally came from Persia. How curious it is that as long ago as the reign of the Roman emperor, Tiberius, walnuts were thought to have special properties and were called "the food of the gods". Almost all the walnuts produced in America are grown in California, mostly from the San Joachim and Sacramento valleys – indeed California produced an astonishing 258,000 tons of walnuts in 1991 alone – and are freshly harvested from September to December.

Nothing that comes from the walnut or its tree is wasted. Quite apart from the food value, walnut shells are used in the manufacture of tyres, for their grip, and also in industrial abrasives. The wood, with its heavy burl, is highly prized as a veneer in furniture manufacture, for example in the dashboards of luxury cars. With our modern concerns for environmentally friendly industry, the walnut sets a wonderful example.

There is much more that could be said about the interesting history of the walnut. But my concern in this book is with other matters. What interests you here and now is how you might incorporate the healthy and nutritious qualities of walnuts into your everyday diet.

CHAPTER TWO

A healthy lifestyle should also be fun

The last thing I want to do is to make you more miserable by inflicting a monotonous and unappetising diet on you and your family. Since the publication of *The Eskimo Diet*, I have made it a general rule to help people not only enjoy good health but to have fun while doing so. While writing the diet and exercises for the remainder of this book I have tried to increase the happiness factor in your life.

There are of course two main reasons why people are interested in diet and exercise, so let's take a good look at what you would like to achieve.

Dieting for the trim figure

Anybody can lose weight, given the right advice and help. There are however certain micro-nutrients you must not exclude from your diet and these can be lost if you indulge in crash dieting or if you attempt to cut out a specific group of foods altogether. If you need more detailed advice on this, consult your doctor or a qualified dietitian or nutritionist. But let me give you a simple example.

Some people worried about cholesterol or adhering to extreme fashion attempt to cut fat entirely from their diets. So they eat no meat, dairy produce, high fat cheeses, nuts, oily fish etc. These people forget that the fat soluble vitamins, such as D and A, and the essential fatty acids are only obtained from fat in the diet. Many women have written to me describing severe skin rashes or hair loss as a result of this dietary imbalance. Even more seriously, I have seen adults develop a softening of their bones, like childhood rickets, from vitamin D deficiency from similar extreme forms of diet. Another young man was described in a medical journal whose hipbone collapsed from simple vitamin C deficiency because he cut vegetables and fruit out of his diet.

To a large extent your daily intake of healthy foods comes down to plain common sense. You know in your heart of hearts when a diet is extreme. Watch out for diets that cut down on a sufficient variety of cereals, fresh fruit, vegetables, dairy produce, fish, meats and vegetable oils. Beware of diets that advocate lengthy fasting or eating just one kind of food for any length of time. So take my advice and balance your diet so as to include as wide a variety of different types of food as possible.

Enough of the warnings – let's get more practical! Here are some tips that will really help you to get that slim, trim figure. So we'll start with the simple mathematics.

Calorie counting

If you eat fewer calories than you burn up through exercise, you lose some of your unwanted fat. The mathematics really are that simple – so simple, it is tempting to overdo things. Certainly it follows that the less you eat, the quicker you will lose weight. Unfortunately there is an overwhelming urge for many slimmers to lose a lot of weight too quickly. They put themselves on horrific diets, often below 1,000 calories per day. Nobody really enjoys this penance and it is virtually impossible to include those important micro-nutrients because the range of foods is simply inadequate. It can damage your health, both physically and psychologically. What's more, it isn't even logical.

Ask anybody why they fail in their slimming attempts and they will often confess that they can lose weight rapidly at first but they cannot keep it up long term. Not to worry, we can quickly learn from this.

To succeed and have fun long term, "gently does it" should be your motto. Don't wait until a few weeks before going on holiday and force yourself to crash diet. Plan your weight reduction over six months or a year. Now, while telling you how to take advantage of this wonderful news about the importance of walnuts, let me give you some helpful tips that have been gleaned from 23 years' hospital experience:

- You are your own individual. Your dietary needs will be different from other people's. So modify your normal diet in such a way that you are still eating the things you love but just less of them.

- The way to find out how much to eat is very simple. Eat what you want in vegetables, fibre and fruit – you can increase these to fill the gap with the reduction in other foods, which will help to avoid hunger. Now spend several weeks testing mild reductions in the high calorie foods such as fats, from meat and dairy produce, and carbohydrate, particularly cakes and chocolate, until you find you are losing half a pound to a pound in weight each week. I am going to put the following in capitals to underline just how important it is.

YOU DON'T NEED TO DIET HARDER THAN THAT. YOU NEED NEVER FEEL THOSE AWFUL HUNGER PANGS THAT RESULT FROM CRASH DIETING AGAIN. YOU WILL FEEL HAPPY AND CONTENTED IN YOURSELF BECAUSE YOU HAVE DISCOVERED THE DIET THAT IS RIGHT FOR YOU NOT JUST FOR DIETING BUT FOR YOUR LONG-TERM HEALTH AND HAPPINESS.

Remember that only half a pound lost per week is a whole 26 pounds in a year. My recipes, menu plan and exercises will make this much easier for you.

- There is a big danger for dieters in too frequent trips to the weighing scales. This only encourages anxiety feelings, which will eventually prove disastrous because anxiety makes you feel hungry and it encourages crash dieting, which nearly always ends in failure. Weigh yourself once a week, always when you first get out of bed. Record your weight on your personal chart and look for long-term gradual weight loss not sudden big falls. If your weight does not fall for a week or so, even if you gain slightly, don't worry. Provided the long-term trend is downwards just stick to your guns. If after a few weeks you find it really has stopped falling, cut back slightly again on your high calorie foods or increase your exercise level slightly and be patient again, following the above routine.
- Now here's another really good tip. Can you remember how your skin becomes hot after exercise? This happens because exercise increases your metabolic rate – the rate at which your internal chemistry burns up calories. So, to help you to burn up calories throughout the rest of the day, plan your exercise routine soon after you get up in the morning. Perhaps you have lost the habit of regular exercise? Or maybe you have arthritis or a heart condition that makes exercise difficult? Don't worry. Anybody, no matter how unfit, disabled or overweight, can find exercises they enjoy and which suit them. It all comes down to your will to succeed. I shall give you plenty of advice on enjoyable exercise in the final chapter of this book.

- If you are concerned about the balance of your diet, ask the advice of a dietitian or nutritionist. They are very friendly and helpful people and often a single visit will sort things out for you.

The heart attack message

No health message could be more vital than one which reduces your risk of having a heart attack. Any dietary advice which reduces this risk is eminently worth taking. That's what makes the Walnut Diet so appealing and relevant.

I am going to show you how to incorporate the walnut message into recipes and an easy to follow 7-day menu plan. But don't worry that any diet against heart attacks is bound to be miserable. Far from it. When I supply the recipes I shall include certain healthy, delicious and highly nutritious foods so you can easily include these in your own fun and healthy menu.

The great message of this book – the message we have received loud and clear from the California Adventists and the research performed at the Loma Linda University of California – is that, with the discovery of the health-giving properties of walnuts, we can help you reduce your cholesterol, and thereby reduce the risk of a heart attack. It only remains for me to show you how to go about it while increasing the variety and pleasure of the food you eat.

CHAPTER THREE

Delicious walnut recipes

Walnut muesli

250g	(8 oz)	rolled oats
125g	(4 oz)	raisins
75g	(3 oz)	walnuts, roughly chopped
50g	(2 oz)	dates, chopped

Mix all ingredients together. Serve with fresh, sliced banana or other fruit if liked.

Serves 6-8.

WALNUT SALADS

Salads are one of the best ways of making full use of the healthy benefits of walnuts.

Walnut and cheese salad

1		large head of crisp lettuce
50g	(2 oz)	California walnuts, roughly chopped
25g	(1 oz)	grated Emmenthal or Cheddar cheese
		freshly ground black pepper

Dressing

1		size 3 egg
2.5g	(½ tsp)	dry mustard

		juice of half a lemon
1clove		garlic, finely crushed
30ml	(2 tbsp)	olive oil
7.5ml	(1½ tsps)	red wine vinegar
7.5g	(1½ tsps)	each fresh chopped chives and parsley

Wash lettuce, tear into bite-sized pieces and place in a bowl with walnuts and cheese. Sprinkle with pepper.

Whisk dressing ingredients together and toss with salad.

Serves 4.

Walnut and seafood salad

250g	(8 oz)	squid, cooked
50g	(2 oz)	prawns, cooked
12		mussels, steamed
2		small heads chicory
250g	(8 oz)	small tomatoes
10		California walnuts
60ml	(4 tbsp)	French dressing

Cut squid into bite-sized pieces. Tear the chicory into pieces and halve the small tomatoes. Combine fish, walnuts, chicory and tomatoes and toss with dressing.

Serves 4.

Walnut rice salad

575g	(1¼ lb)	rice, cooked

Dressing

5ml	(1 tsp)	vinegar
45ml	(3 tbsp)	olive oil mixed with ½ tsp sugar and a pinch of salt

Half		a cucumber, cubed
1		small carrot, grated
2		size 3 eggs, hardboiled and chopped
100g	(4 oz)	cooked ham, cut into strips
75g	(3 oz)	Edam cheese, cubed
10		California walnuts

Sliced tomatoes and parsley to garnish

Mix together rice and dressing, add cucumber, carrot, chopped egg, ham, cheese and walnuts. Pile into a serving dish and garnish with tomato slices and chopped parsley.

Serves 4.

Grilled mushroom salad

		large pinch each dried rosemary and thyme
		large pinch freshly ground black pepper
30ml	(2 tbps)	olive oil
2		shallots or 1 small Spanish onion, very finely chopped
12		large flat mushrooms, stalks removed
2		small crisp lettuces, washed
100g	(4 oz)	green beans, trimmed, cut up & lightly cooked until 'al dente'
50g	(2 oz)	Gruyere or Emmenthal cheese, grated
100g	(2 oz)	California walnuts, coarsely chopped
1		lemon, cut into wedges
2		small tomatoes, quartered, to garnish

Mix together herbs, pepper, oil and shallots and marinade mushrooms in this to 10-15 minutes. Cook mushrooms under a hot grill for 2 minutes each side, remove from heat and cool slightly. Arrange lettuce leaves in 4 small bowls or cups and place mushrooms on top. Cover with green beans and sprinkle over cheese and chopped walnuts. Garnish with lemon wedges and tomato quarters.

Serve with lemon vinaigrette.

Serves 4.

BREAD, CAKES, PUDDINGS AND BISCUITS

Walnut stollen

450g	(1 lb)	strong plain flour (for breadmaking)	
5g	(1 tsp)	salt	
5g	(1 tsp)	sugar	
75g	(3 oz)	margarine, high in polyunsaturates	
1		sachet fast action dried yeast	
175g	(6 oz)	California walnuts (chopped)	
100g	(4 oz)	sultanas	soaked overnight in 30ml (2 tbsp) rum
100g	(4 oz)	raisins	
50g	(2 oz)	chopped peel	
225ml	(8 fl oz)	warm milk	
1		size 3 egg, beaten	
		melted butter	
75g	(3 oz)	glacé cherries (chopped)	
15g	(1 tbsp)	sugar plus 2 x 15g (2 tbsp) hot water for glazing	
		icing sugar, for dusting	

Place flour, salt and sugar in a bowl, rub in the margarine and stir in the yeast. Add the chopped walnuts and fruit soaked in rum, work in the warmed milk and beaten egg.
Turn dough onto a lightly floured surface and knead until smooth

and no longer sticky. Place the dough in a lightly oiled polythene bag, tied loosely, and leave until it has risen and doubled in size.

Divide dough in half and shape each half into an oval 30cm x 20 cm (12 in x 8 in). Brush surface of each half with melted butter. Spread with glacé cherries then fold over and press lightly together.

Place both cakes on a floured baking sheet and leave to prove in a warm place until doubled in size.

Bake in a moderate oven 180°C, 350°F, Gas No. 3 for 40-45 minutes. Remove from the oven and while still hot brush with sugar and water glaze. Dust with icing sugar when cold.

Makes two stollen.

NB Stollen can be frozen or stored for up to 10 days in an airtight container.

Banana walnut bread

75g	(3 oz)	margarine, high in polyunsaturates
175g	(6 oz)	sugar
4g	(¾ tsp)	grated lemon rind
1		size 3 egg
150	(5 oz)	plain flour
75g	(3 oz)	California walnuts, finely ground
7½g	(1½ tsp)	baking powder
1½g	(¼ tsp)	bicarbonate of soda
3		medium sized ripe bananas, mashed
50g	(2 oz)	California walnuts, chopped

Cream together margarine, sugar and rind. Beat in egg. Combine flour, ground walnuts, baking powder and bicarbonate of soda. Add this to creamed mixture, alternately with bananas, blending thoroughly after each addition. Stir in chopped walnuts. Pour into greased 22cm x 10cm (2 lb) deep loaf tin.

Bake in moderate oven 177°C, 375°F, Gas No. 4 for 50 to 60 minutes, until it is golden brown and a skewer inserted in centre comes out clean.

Turn out and cool on a wire tray.

Makes 1 loaf (10 slices).

Avocado walnut muffins

1		size 2 egg
50g	(2 oz)	sugar
1 300-350g	(10-12 oz)	soft, ripe avocado, peeled and mashed
225g	(8 oz)	self-raising flour, sieved
125ml	(5 fl oz)	semi-skimmed milk
175g	(6 oz)	California walnuts
50g	(2 oz)	mature Cheddar cheese, grated

Beat the egg and sugar together in a bowl. Gently fold in avocado alternately with flour, milk, 100g (4 oz) of the walnuts and the cheese until combined. Spoon mixture into 12-15 well-greased and floured deep muffin tins and top with remaining walnuts. Bake in a moderate oven 180°C, 350°F, Gas No. 4 for 25-35 minutes.

Makes 12-15 muffins.

Variation

Spoon mixture into a well-greased and floured 24cm x 10cm deep (2lb deep) loaf tin. Bake for 50-60 minutes or until a skewer inserted in centre comes out clean.

Coffee walnut torte

Torte

275g	(10 oz)	California walnuts, finely ground
4		size 2 eggs
100g	(4 oz)	caster sugar
5ml	(1 tsp)	baking powder

Coffee cream

50g	(2 oz)	California walnuts, finely ground
50g	(2 oz)	dark cooking chocolate
300ml	(½ pt)	whipping or double cream
10ml	(2 tsp)	coffee powder
15g	(1 tbsp)	caster sugar
		Fresh raspberries to decorate

Beat egg yolks and sugar together in a bowl until pale and creamy. In a separate bowl, beat egg whites until stiff but not dry. Lightly fold together the yolk mixture, egg whites, baking powder and walnuts. Pour mixture into a greased and lined 22cm (7½ in) loose bottomed tin. Bake in a moderate oven 160°C, 325°F, Gas No. 3 for 40-50 minutes, until it leaves pan sides or feels firm when pressed gently with the fingertips. Remove and cool.

Grate chocolate finely and mix with ground walnuts. Beat cream to firm peaks, fold in coffee and sugar.

Split cake across and fill with some of the coffee cream, spreading remainder around top and sides. Press walnut mixture around sides and decorate top with fresh raspberries.

Serves 6-8.

Christmas walnut pudding

225g	(8 oz)	raisins, chopped
225g	(8 oz)	sultanas
225g	(8 oz)	currants
50g	(2 oz)	mixed cut peel
100g	(4 oz)	California walnuts, roughly chopped
45ml	(3 tbsp)	brandy or milk
200g	(7 oz)	margarine, high in polyunsaturates
200g	(7 oz)	soft brown sugar
2		size 3 eggs, beaten
2½ ml	½ tsp	each, mixed spice, ground ginger, nutmeg and cinnamon
175g	(6 oz)	plain flour
175g	(6 oz)	fresh breadcrumbs
		grated rind and juice of 1 lemon
15ml	(1 tbsp)	black treacle
45-60ml	(3-4 tbsp)	beer or milk

In a large bowl, mix together fruits, peel and walnuts. Pour over brandy, cover and leave for 1-2 hours, or overnight if possible. Add all remaining ingredients to the fruit mixture and mix very thoroughly, adding more milk if necessary, to a dropping consistency.

Place mixture in a large greased 1 kg (2½ lb) pudding basin. Cover with lid or greaseproof paper and two layers of foil. Steam in a large saucepan of gently boiling water for 5 hours, topping up with boiling water regularly, as necessary.

Either turn out and serve, or cool, re-cover and store in a cool, dry place until required. Steam again for 2-3 hours before serving or microwave according to manufacturer's instructions.

Serve with brandy sauce.

Serves 8-10.

NB Christmas puddings are best made 1-2 months in advance for the flavour to mature.

Walnut refrigerator cookies

225g	(8 oz)	margarine, high in polyunsaturates
225g	(8 oz)	white cooking fat, high in polyunsaturates
225g	(8 oz)	soft brown sugar
225g	(8 oz)	granulated sugar
3		size 2 eggs
725g	(1lb 10oz)	plain flour
5g	(1 tsp)	bicarbonate of soda sieved together with
10-15g	(2-3 tsp)	cinnamon
225g	(8 oz)	California walnuts, roughly chopped
2		egg whites, slightly beaten, for brushing
		California walnuts, chopped into pieces for topping

Cream together margarine, white cooking fat and sugars. Beat in eggs until well blended. Add flour mixture gradually to creamed mixture, add chopped walnuts and mix well. Divide dough into 4 equal parts and shape each into a log about 6 cm (2 in) in diameter. Wrap logs separately in waxed paper or plastic wrap and chill overnight. With a sharp knife, slice logs into rounds about 1 cm (¼ inch) thick. Place rounds well apart on greased baking sheets, brush lightly with beaten egg white and top each with walnut pieces.

Bake in a moderately hot oven, 190°C, 375°F, Gas No. 5 for 15-20 minutes until golden around the edges. Cool on a wire tray.

Makes 90-100 cookies.

NB Cookie rolls can be stored in the refrigerator for up to a week, or in the freezer for up to three months.

Walnut delights

50g	(2 oz)	rolled oats
50g	(2 oz)	desiccated coconut
175g	(6 oz)	plain flour, sieved
175g	(6 oz)	caster sugar
50g	(2 oz)	California walnuts, coarsely chopped
50g	(2 oz)	margarine, high in polyunsaturates
15ml	(1 tbsp)	golden syrup
7.5g	(1½ tsp)	bicarbonate of soda
30ml	(2 tbsp)	boiling water
5-10ml	(1-2 tsp)	semi-skimmed milk, if required, to bind
50g	(2 oz)	California walnuts, finely ground, to coat

Mix together oats, coconut, flour, sugar and chopped walnuts in a bowl. Melt margarine and golden syrup in a pan.

Mix bicarbonate of soda with boiling water, add to margarine mixture.

Pour this into dry ingredients, mixing well and pressing together with fingertips. Add a little milk, if necessary, to bind dough. Shape into teaspoon-sized balls. Roll balls in finely ground walnuts and place well apart on greased baking sheets. Bake in a very moderate oven 163°C, 325°F, Gas No. 3 for 15-20 minutes. Cool slightly, then remove and cool on wire trays.

Makes 30-40.

Walnut and raisin muffins

225g	(8 oz)	self-raising flour
100g	(4 oz)	bran
50g	(2 oz)	wheatgerm
1¼g	(¼ tsp)	salt
3.75g	(¾ tsp)	bicarbonate of soda
225ml	(8 fl oz)	low-fat yoghurt
300ml	(½ pt)	semi-skimmed milk
50g	(2 oz)	black treacle
25g	(1 oz)	margarine
50g	(2 oz)	raisins
50g	(2 oz)	California walnuts, roughly chopped
		Good pinch of cinnamon or mixed spice (optional)

Combine dry ingredients into a mixing bowl. Mix together yoghurt and milk. Heat black treacle and margarine gently in pan until melted. Allow to cool. Mix raisins and walnuts with dry ingredients then add the cooled treacle mixture. Beat well together until smooth. Place spoonfuls of mixture in greased patty tins and bake in a hot oven 220°C, 425°F, Gas No. 7 for 15-20 minutes until well risen and golden brown. Serve warm.

Makes 20-24 muffins.

Cheese and walnut loaf

225g	(8 oz)	self-raising flour
5g	(1 tsp)	baking powder
5g	(1 tsp)	dry mustard
2½g	(½ tsp)	salt
1¼g	(¼ tsp)	pepper
75g	(3 oz)	margarine
50g	(2 oz)	Edam cheese, grated
50g	(2 oz)	walnuts, roughly chopped
150ml	(¼ pt)	semi-skimmed milk
1		egg, size 2

Sieve dry ingredients together in a bowl, add remaining ingredients and beat together with a wooden spoon until well mixed (2-3 minutes). Place the mixture in a greased and bottom-lined ½ kg (1 lb) loaf tin and smooth top. Bake in a pre-heated oven 190°C, 375°F, Gas No. 5 for 45-50 minutes. Leave in tin for 5 minutes, then turn out to cool. Serve cold, sliced and lightly spread with margarine.

DINNER RECIPES USING WALNUTS

Mushroom and walnut stir-fry

15ml	(1 tbsp)	vegetable oil, high in polyunsaturates
50g	(2 oz)	California walnuts
½		red pepper sliced
100g	(4 oz)	mange-tout peas
225g	(8 oz)	oyster mushrooms or large white, flat mushrooms, stalks removed and sliced
45ml	(3 tbsp)	orange juice

Heat oil in a wok or large frying pan and fry the walnuts until golden brown. Add the peppers, mange-tout peas, mushrooms and orange juice and stir-fry quickly for 2-3 minutes.

Serve immediately.

Serve as a vegetarian meal or to accompany poultry or fish.

Serves 2-3.

Vegetable and walnut bake

225g	(8 oz)	baby carrots or carrots cut into thin sticks 6cm long, cooked 5-7 minutes, until 'al dente'
225g	(8 oz)	broccoli florets, cooked 3-4 minutes, until 'al dente'
225g	(8 oz)	small tomatoes
225g	(8 oz)	aubergine, sliced and salted for 30 minutes, then blanched in boiling water for 1 minute
225g	(8 oz)	small or pickling onions, peeled and cooked 8-10 minutes until 'al dente'
15g	(1 oz)	margarine, high in polyunsaturates
15g	(1 oz)	plain flour
300ml	(½ pt)	semi-skimmed milk
300ml	(½ pt)	vegetable water
		salt and papper
		pinch dry mustard
50g	(2 oz)	Cheddar cheese, grated
50g	(2 oz)	California walnuts

Arrange the carrots, broccoli, tomatoes, aubergine and onions in rows in a large 30cm x 20cm (12 in x 8 in) ovenproof dish. Melt the margarine in a saucepan and add the flour. Cook for one minute over a low heat. Remove from heat and slowly add the water in which vegetables were cooked, together with milk, salt, pepper and mustard. Return to heat, stirring all the time, and bring to the boil. Add the cheese and pour over vegetables. Sprinkle the walnuts over the top, cover the dish and bake in a hot oven 200°C, 400°F, Gas No. 6 for 20 minutes, then remove cover and bake for a further 10 minutes until the top is lightly browned and the vegetables are cooked.

Serve as a vegetarian meal or accompaniment to meat.

Serves 4-6.

Szechuan walnut chicken

4		chicken breasts each weighing about 175g (6 oz), cut into cubes
30g	(2 tbsp)	cornflour
		vegetable oil, high in polyunsaturates, for frying
1		medium onion, peeled and sliced
2		cloves garlic, chopped
100g	(4 oz)	California walnuts
30ml	(2 tbsp)	dry white wine or medium dry sherry
15ml	(1 tbsp)	soya sauce
5ml	(1 tsp)	chili bean paste (or to taste)
2.5g	(½ tsp)	sugar
100g	(4 oz)	mange-tout peas
1		medium red pepper, cut into fine strips

Coat chicken lightly in cornflour. Heat 45ml (3 tbsp) oil in a wok or deep frying pan, fry chicken until golden then remove from pan. Pour off any excess oil, leaving about 1 tbsp in wok. Stir-fry onion, garlic and walnuts for one minute. Add wine or sherry, bean paste and sugar. Return chicken, stir, cover and cook over medium heat for 5 minutes or until tender. Add vegetables, warm through for 1 minute.

Serve with boiled rice.

Serves 4.

Crab fish cakes

2 170-225g	(6-8 oz)	cans crabmeat
or		
350-450g	(¾-1 lb)	crab sticks, sliced thinly
350g	(3/4 lb)	potatoes, cooked and mashed with
30ml	(2 tbsp)	milk and
15g	(1 oz)	margarine, high in polyunsaturates
25g	(1 oz)	spring onions or chives, very finely chopped
50g	(2 oz)	California walnuts, chopped
100g	(4 oz)	fresh breadcrumbs
1		size 3 egg
1		size 3 egg white
		large pinch of salt

Mix together in a bowl the crabmeat, potatoes, spring onions, half the walnuts, half the breadcrumbs, the egg, egg white and salt. Divide into 8, form into balls and flatten. Mix together remaining walnuts and breadcrumbs and coat the patties. Shallow fry in a non-stick pan, brushed with oil for 8-10 minutes, turning once or dot with margarine and grill under medium heat for 10-15 minutes, turning once.

Serves 4 (8 fish cakes).

Fish cutlets á l'orange

4x150g	(5 oz)	haddock, cod or monkfish cutlets
2		medium oranges
45ml	(3 tbsp)	Grand Marnier, Cointreau or other orange liqueur
300ml	(½ pt)	fresh orange juice
100g	(4 oz)	California walnuts
30ml	(2 tbsp)	lemon juice
45ml	(3 tbsp)	fresh mint, finely chopped
		freshly ground pepper to taste

Using a vegetable peeler, remove orange skins and cut into thin strips. Cut away all white pith and dice or cut oranges into segments. Simmer liqueur, orange juice and rind together in a frying pan for 10-15 minutes until liquid is reduced to about 3 tablespoons. Add remaining ingredients and reheat.
Grill, bake or barbecue fish and serve with the relish, new potatoes and a tossed green salad.

Serves 4.

Easy beef and walnut casserole

15ml	(1 tbsp)	oil
450g	(1 lb)	lean braising steak, cubed
100g	(4 oz)	onions, peeled and chopped
225g	(8 oz)	mushrooms, washed and sliced
100g	(4 oz)	fennel, chopped
300ml	(½ pt)	stock
150ml	(¼ pt)	red wine
		bouquet garni
		salt and pepper
15g	(½ oz)	flour
50g	(2 oz)	California walnuts, roughly chopped

Heat oil and fry the beef until just brown. Add onions and mushrooms and cook until lightly browned. Add fennel, red wine, stock, bouquet garni and seasoning. Place in a casserole dish with tight-fitting lid and cook in a moderate oven 175°C, 350°F, Gas No. 4 for 2 hours. Blend flour with a little water, add to casserole with walnuts and return to oven for a further 15 to 20 minutes.

Serves 4.

Chicken Koresht

1 kg	(2lb 2 oz)	chicken thigh joints, weight approximate
15g	(1 tbsp)	ground cumin
10g	(2 tspn)	turmeric
2½g	(½ tsp)	ground black pepper
30ml	(2 tbsp)	vegetable oil, high in polyunsaturates
1x400g	(14 oz)	can whole peeled tomatoes
150ml	(5 fl oz)	chicken stock
1		onion peeled and chopped
4		dates, roughly chopped
½		lemon, sliced
2		dried limes, optional

Walnut paste

100g	(4 oz)	California walnuts
10		large leaves basil or parsley
10g	(2 tsp)	ground cumin
10g	(2 tsp)	cinnamon
150ml	(5 fl oz)	natural yoghurt

Combine spices in a bowl and coat chicken joints. Heat oil in a deep heavy-based pan and fry chicken, turning once, until golden. Add remaining casserole ingredients, cover and simmer for 45 minutes. Allow to cool and leave overnight, if possible for flavours to develop.

Walnut paste

Liquidise paste ingredients together until combined and forming a coarsely chopped texture.

Reheat chicken thoroughly and cook for a further 15-20 minutes until tender. Serve chicken with the walnut paste and boiled rice.

Serves 4-6.

Bean and walnut pasta

325g	(12 oz)	penne or other pasta shapes
30ml	(2 tbsp)	olive oil
100g	(4 oz)	lean smoked bacon, chopped
100g	(4 oz)	California walnuts
300ml	(½ pt)	strong chicken stock
3		medium tomatoes, roughly chopped
400g	(14 oz)	can canellini, lima or borlotti beans, rinsed and drained
10-15		large basil leaves, or parsley, chopped

Cook pasta in plenty of lightly salted boiled water until just cooked – 'al dente'. Drain and set aside. Heat oil in a large pan and fry bacon and walnuts for 2-3 minutes. Stir in stock and tomatoes, simmer for 1-2 minutes. Toss in pasta, beans and basil or parsley and heat thoroughly. Season with freshly ground pepper.

Serve with freshly grated Parmesan cheese.

Serves 4.

NON-WALNUT RECIPES FOR THE MENU PLAN

Mackerel baked potatoes

225g	(8 oz)	smoked mackerel fillets, skinned
15ml	(1 tbsp)	horseradish sauce (optional)
		salt and freshly ground pepper
		a little skimmed milk
2 225g	(8 oz)	potatoes, baked in the oven
30g	(1 oz)	low to medium-fat cheese, grated

Flake the mackerel into a bowl and mix in the horseradish sauce, if using, seasoning and a little milk. Cut open the potatoes and fill with the fish mixture. Cook under a preheated medium grill until the mackerel is hot. Sprinkle over the grated cheese and return to the grill until the cheese has melted. Serve hot.

Serves 2.

Oaty burgers

450g	(1 lb)	lean minced beef
50g	(2 oz)	rolled oats
1		egg
75ml	(3 tbsp)	tomato sauce
4		wholemeal burger buns

Mix all ingredients together, using egg to bind mixture. Use a small amount of flour to shape burgers. Lightly grill for approximately 4 minutes each side. Serve in a warmed bun with a large mixed salad.

Makes 4.

Chicken stir-fry with wildgrain rice

100g	(4 oz)	raw chicken breast, finely sliced
15ml	(1 tbsp)	each of sherry, tomato purée, soya sauce
50g	(2 oz)	mushrooms, sliced
1		onion, sliced
1		stick celery, sliced
1		small clove garlic, sliced (optional)
50g	(2 oz)	beansprouts
10ml	(2 tsp)	sunflower oil

Heat oil in a large, heavy-based frying pan or wok and cook chicken. Add vegetables and garlic, if using, cook for a further 1-2 minutes. Mix together the sherry, tomato purée and soya sauce and add to the pan. Heat through and serve with rice.

Serves 1.

Tuna and mackerel risotto

200g	(7 oz)	tin tuna in brine, drained and flaked
1		small smoked mackerel fillet, skinned and flaked
1		packet savoury rice
1		each onion, courgette, pepper, chopped
100g	(4 oz)	mushrooms, chopped
10ml	(2 tsp)	olive oil

Cook savoury rice according to instructions. Gently sauté vegetables in olive oil, add tuna and mackerel and heat through. Mix with hot rice and serve in bowls topped with freshly ground black pepper and chopped parsley.

Serves 2.

Beany pasta bake

400g	(14 oz)	tin mixed beans in chili sauce
400g	(14 oz)	tin chopped tomatoes
1		onion, chopped
100g	(4 oz)	dried pasta shapes
120g	(5 oz)	tin sweetcorn, drained
10ml	(2 tsp)	olive oil
1 tbsp		Parmesan cheese, grated

Cook onion and sweetcorn in olive oil. Add the tomatoes and mixed beans and cook on a low heat for 5-10 minutes. Cook pasta in plenty of boiling water, drain and stir into bean mixture. Pile into an ovenproof dish, sprinkle with Parmesan cheese and grill until browned.

Serves 2.

CHAPTER FOUR

Putting the walnut diet into practice

I have assumed that most people wishing to use the Walnut Diet will use it as part of a weight control and fitness programme. This is why I have based the following menu plan on 1500 calories daily. The meals have been varied to make them as enjoyable as possible while enabling you to take advantage of important health-giving foods and keeping to pleasant and healthy balance. If you wish to eat healthily while not reducing weight, simply modify the plan to accommodate your normal dietary level of intake. As a guide, a healthy young man will often eat about 2,400 calories as his normal and a woman 2,100. If, on the other hand you are struggling to lose weight even at 1500 calories a day, reduce little by little below this.

Take my advice and avoid falling to levels below 1100 calories daily since, below this, it is difficult to ensure a balanced diet including those essential micro-nutrients.

Anyone contemplating such a strict diet should obtain the advice of a dietitian or nutritionist.

THE WALNUT DIET 7-DAY MENU PLAN

Daily Allowance

The following should be taken daily to maintain a healthy diet:

20g	(4/5 oz)	low fat spread
450ml	(¾ pint)	semi-skimmed milk

in addition to fresh fruit; choose any two of the following:

1 pear, 1 apple, 1 banana, 1 nectarine, 1 peach, 12 grapes, portion of strawberries, blackberries, raspberries, plus 1 diet yoghurt or fromage frais.

- Lunch and evening meal are interchangeable.
- Fresh fruit portion can be taken as snacks instead of desserts.
- Low calorie squashes and fizzy drinks can be taken freely.
- Tea and coffee with sweetener (with milk from allowance) can be taken throughout the day.
- Breakfasts are interchangeable except for day 7.

Day 1

Breakfast: Walnut muesli (see recipe) with milk from allowance

Lunch: Mackerel baked potatoes with fresh tomatoes (see recipe)
Portion of fresh fruit from daily allowance

Dinner: 1 oaty burger in a wholemeal burger bun with a large mixed salad (see recipe)
Portion of fresh fruit from daily allowance

Day 2

Breakfast: 2 Shredded Wheat and milk from allowance

Lunch: Small tin of baked beans with two slices of wholemeal toast
Fresh fruit from allowance

Dinner: Easy beef and walnut casserole (see recipe) with 150g (6 oz.) boiled potatoes and fresh steamed broccoli
Fruit from allowance

Day 3

Breakfast: 2 Weetabix with milk from allowance

Lunch: Walnut and cheese salad with 2 granary rolls
Fruit from allowance

Dinner: Chicken stir-fry with 150g (6 oz) wildgrain rice (see recipe)
Portion of fresh fruit topped with diet yoghurt or fromage frais

Day 4

Breakfast: 1 toasted wholemeal muffin with marmalade and a large glass of fresh orange juice

Lunch: Ham and salad sandwich, made with two small slices of bread
Fresh fruit from allowance

Dinner: Tuna and mackerel risotto (see recipe)
Fresh fruit with fromage frais from allowance

Day 5

Breakfast: serving of Bran Flakes with milk from allowance and a few sultanas to sweeten

Lunch: 4 walnut muffins (see recipe) with 100g (4 oz) low fat cream cheese
A small serving of grapes

Dinner: Beany pasta bake (see recipe)
Mandarin oranges (canned in own juice) in sugar-free jelly

Day 6

Breakfast: Boiled egg with 1 slice of wholemeal toast and 2 teaspoons of marmalade

Lunch: Tuna-filled pitta bread. (mix 3oz tuna in brine with a dessertspoon of reduced calorie mayonnaise and black pepper. Pile into pitta bread with shredded lettuce and slices of cucumber and tomato)
Fresh fruit

Dinner: Mushroom and Walnut Stir Fry with 100g (4 oz dried weight) noodles (see recipe)
Fresh fruit with a little low-fat fromage frais

Day 7

Breakfast: 2 small slices of toast with 2 slices of lean, grilled bacon

Lunch: Granary roll filled with lots of mixed salad
Fresh fruit portion

Dinner: 3 slices lean roast beef with 200g (8 oz) roast potatoes (roasted in sunflower oil). Fresh vegetables and a small portion of gravy which has been skimmed of fat
Small portion of fruit crumble with a little custard or yoghurt
1 glass of red or white wine

CHAPTER FIVE

The exercise plan

Exercise is an important ingredient in any weight reducing health-promoting programme. And how wonderfully pleasurable and invigorating it can be, provided we choose an exercise that we really enjoy.

Feeling good in mind and body

We all know instinctively that when we are physically fit and exercising regularly we feel better. There are times when we should believe what our instincts are telling us. There is no doubt that people who exercise regularly tend to have lower weights, less fat, a lower heart rate in response to exercise, and tend to be fitter generally for all of the demands of the modern working day. But we have all heard of joggers who die from heart attacks out on the roads and parks. So does exercise really do our health any good?

The answer is yes. But it has to be regular and in sufficient amount.

Exercise and your heart

There is a lot of evidence now that exercise and blood fats are closely related. Exercise raises the beneficial HDL cholesterol and it lowers the other high risk blood fat, called triglyceride. At the same time it burns off calories and helps keep down your weight. There is also evidence that exercise also reduces your risk of a heart attack.

So here are a few tips

The right exercise for you should be fun. It should make you feel good in mind and body. It might even help you make some new friends and improve the quality of your life.

But a word of caution: If you are overweight or not too fit, don't suddenly start performing difficult and strenuous exercise. The motto, as with dieting, is *gently does it.*

What level of exercise do I recommend?

What will be fine for a relatively fit young woman will not suit an obese sixty-year-old man. But I do believe that anybody, even the disabled – perhaps especially the disabled – will be able to find some regular exercise that will suit them. The best kind of exercises for this purpose use the big muscles of the legs and will give rise to a reasonable increase in heart rate. These include light running, jogging or brisk walking. If this kind of exercise causes pain, for instance angina, I would not recommend it. If all of these are impossible because you are either disabled or have bad angina or your legs are affected by arthritis or intermittent claudication (the cramp caused by narrowing of the arteries to the legs), then light floor exercises at home or in your local gymnasium is a really excellent alternative. Another alternative, which gives you the chance to make friends and enjoy yourself, is swimming. People with a weight problem or a disability that rules out other forms of exercise will often find they can manage this. But it has to be regular and planned if it is to really do you good.

Whatever form of exercise you choose, remember to start gently and build up slowly. If running for instance, only run half a mile or so at your ease and stop as often as you need for a breather or to relieve cramps in your legs. A similar build-up applies to swimming or gymnasium exercises. It is far more important to develop a regular routine you enjoy than to try to force the pace and put yourself in the wrong frame of mind ever after.

A philosophy for any age

One of the commonest objections to taking regular exercise is the cry: But I'm too old, Doctor. Not a bit of it! There is no age limit to the beneficial effects of regular exercise. Haven't you long suspected that some of the unhealthy developments of ageing are really the consequences of lifestyle more than the effects of age itself? Fitness is a philosophy for any age.

Recently I watched a group of elderly men and women perform floor exercises in a central London gymnasium. The oldest was more than ninety years old and many suffered from arthritis or heart disease – some even had new hip joints. What was more they seemed to enjoy themselves tremendously.

The cardinal rules

- Choose an exercise that will stretch you a little without overdoing it.
- Choose an exercise you will enjoy long term.
- If possible, choose an exercise in which you join in with a group of friends. Group exercise is a wonderful way of getting together and making friends, for young and elderly alike.
- Start gently and build up to a level that stretches you without overdoing it.

Now let's look at the types of exercise you can choose from.

Choice of exercises

One of the marvellous things about exercise is the very wide range of choices. There will be one or more that anybody would enjoy doing. Broadly speaking, exercises can be divided into two categories, "outdoor", which roughly equates with natural and under which category I would include swimming, and "indoor", which includes gymnasium, floor exercises and the use of exercise equipment.

Outdoor exercise

Many people regularly take exercise as part of their leisure, for example by participating in team games such as football, cricket, rugby, hockey, netball, basketball, volleyball and rounders. These are highly recommended since they make exercise fun and help to promote human contacts and friendship. Others will prefer individual sports such as golf, crown bowling, tennis and squash, which are just as satisfying and good for health and fitness. They are all to be highly recommended.

However many other people prefer to take their exercise in ways other than competitive sport and I shall concentrate on these alternatives.

Walking

Walking is the most natural exercise of all. It can also be very enjoyable. I believe that part of the explanation for our present epidemic of heart attacks is the profound life-style changes ushered in by the car and the ease of public transport. Most of us walk a good deal less than our grandparents.

Walking keeps you active and mobile. It can help relieve stress and tension and, as a regular feature in your lifestyle, it will burn up those excess calories, helping to keep your weight at a healthy level. The key is "regular".

Swimming

Swimming is a favourite of mine since it is so easy to modify to suit your degree of fitness. It is often the exercise of choice if you are overweight or disabled, because the buoyancy of the water makes you lighter. It is the ideal exercise for stamina, strength and suppleness, particularly if you plan to vary the strokes so you use many different muscles.

As with any exercise, it is most fun if you swim with friends. Often, with the more modern swimming pools, you will find pleasant changing facilities and fun amenities for children.

Cycling

Cycling is an excellent form of exercise, tougher than walking or swimming, and will really help burn up those excess calories. It really comes into its own in a rural environment and can be a great way of enjoying the countryside. You will find lots of clubs and groups who organise day trips, or even weekend breaks and holidays.

I must admit to reservations about cycling in busy towns or cities, unless adequate provision has been made towards safety by the road planning authority. Parents should be particularly cautious about allowing children to cycle on or near busy roads.

Many people find it convenient to have a cycling machine in their homes so they can conveniently exercise in private. This is a good way to tone up the muscles of your legs and helps burn up calories. Since it largely tones up the leg muscles, it works best as part of a more general programme of exercise aimed at toning up the rest of your body.

Jogging and running

Let's get it clear straight away that for most people there is no need to exercise at this planned level. A regular walk or a swim will more than suffice. But some people like to plan a tougher routine which really does stretch them. It can be fun, provided you don't become too obsessional about it, and is a very effective way of getting and staying fit – but I should warn you that you need to be reasonably fit to tolerate it.

Practical tip: if you are a woman, do not jog, walk or cycle alone. Enjoy your outings with a friend or join an athletic club and do it as part of a group.

Other alternatives

Virtually any sport which involves walking, running, or vigorous use of the limbs is fine provided you enjoy it and it is sensible enough for you to accommodate it without distress.

Indoor exercises

Floor aerobics

What is the meaning of "aerobic exercise"?

We have all heard the term "aerobic" used in relation to exercise so what does this mean? If you really sprint hard you tire quickly and at the end of the sprint you will find yourself very much out of breath with a heart pumping uncomfortably fast in your chest. What you have done is to exercise too fast for the oxygen arriving at your muscles. The muscles have gone on contracting hard even without oxygen but you pay for it when you stop. This is called "an-aerobic" exercise and is clearly very heavy exercise indeed. If, on the other hand, your exercise is lighter, such as a brisk walk or light floor exercises, then the oxygen can arrive at your muscles as quickly as they need it. You are much less breathless and your muscles will be a good deal less exhausted. This is termed "aerobic" exercise.

I would like to devote some space and time to these at-home aerobic exercises since they are fun and very popular. There are many examples of floor exercises on popular videos. If you are considering these, I would suggest you find a presenter and a range of exercises that you feel comfortable with.

Will I need special equipment?

For the exercises I have prepared for you, you won't need complex pieces of exercise equipment – though I have no objection to a small trampoline for jogging or an exercise bicycle for trimming and moulding the hips and thighs. But let me give you a small practical tip.

Do your ankles and knees ache when you do even light exercises? Cut out two pieces of spongy rubberised carpet underlay, each a yard square and lay them on top of one another to give you a nice springy base that will help protect your ankle joints.

Floor exercises improve muscle tone, suppleness, help your waistline and give you an exhilarating sense of being fit and on top of the world. It is much more fun if you perform these to popular music. A good beat is essential – test tunes until you find one with a good one-and-two-and-one-and-two rhythm.

I would recommend that you perform these exercises early in your day, usually at a convenient regular time, so they boost your metabolism rate and help burn up calories throughout the rest of the day.

Stretching

Stand on your mat with ankles together and arms by your sides and, to a simple one-and-two beat, lightly clap your hands at stretch above your head while jumping so your two feet are widely spaced, then bring your feet together again and your hands back down to your sides. This exercise should be repeated to a "one-and-two" beat or rhythm, with one for hands up and two for by your side, for one minute before changing to your next exercise step. At first perform ten, later increase to twenty.

Waist Stretch: light exercise

Stand with legs apart and arms outstretched level with your shoulders. Now twist to your left over the pace of one-and-two, then back to the start position for one-and-two, then twist to your right with the same rhythm, one-and-two, and then back to the start again for one-and-two. Again, start with ten and later increase to twenty.

With practice and increasing fitness, you will find you can stretch yourself a little harder – but do be careful with twisting and stretching exercises and avoid overdoing it. These are intended to be light only.

Allow one and a half minutes, then a short breather.

Waist Stretch 2: harder exercise

This is more difficult and may not be possible if you are greatly overweight or unfit to start with. Try to work up to it using the lighter exercises.

Kneel with knees apart, your hips pushed forwards, and your arms above your head. Now, to that same one-and-two rhythm, twist and reach behind you so your right hand touches your left heel, then back to start position. Then repeat, following that same rhythm, so your left hand touches your right heel. Start with ten and later increase to twenty touches in all.

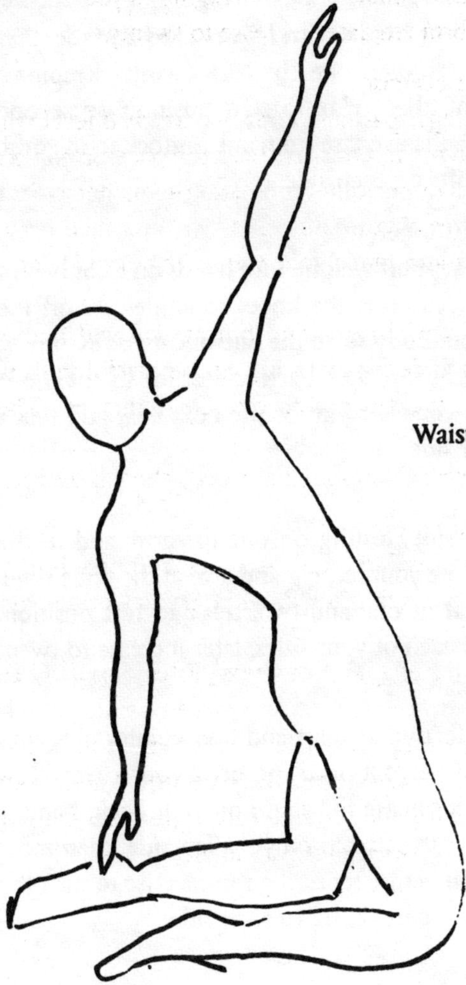

Waist Stretch 2

Waist toner exercises

The following exercises are graded in order of severity. Most people will easily manage exercises 1 and 2 but only a younger or fitter person should attempt exercise 3.

Waist toner 1

Sit on a chair or bench with legs relaxed and together, then to one-and-two, elevate one buttock while keeping spine reasonably upright, then relax to start position on second one-and-two. Alternate the exercise from one buttock to the other over one minute. Ten lifts on each side.

Alternative to waist toner 1

Sit on floor, support weight with hands on floor behind your back, bend your legs up at the knees so ankles are off the floor and then rotate your body so, to the one-and-two rhythm, you roll over onto your right hip, then back to rest for the next one-and-two, then over to your left hip for the next beat and repeat. Ten exercises to either side.

Waist toner 2

Lie on your side, resting on one forearm, and to the beat, one-and-two, elevate your left leg and arm at the same time. Then to the second beat of one-and-two, relax to rest position. Start with ten times on each of your sides, later increase to twenty.

Waist toner 3

Stand with feet wide apart and toes comfortably outwards, straighten arms above your head and bend your knees. Now, with your hips forwards to ease the strain on your back, bend to your right until you feel the stretch on your left side, then move back to the start position before repeating the exercise to the other side. You should do twelve in all, six to each side.

Waist toner 4

With feet about shoulders' width apart in a relaxed stance, squat until knees are roughly half bent, then alternately touch right toes with left hand and left toes with right hand. This is a fairly fast exercise. The "one" of the one-and-two rhythm should be left toes and the "two" right toes. Twelve touches to either side.

Bust toners

The most vigorous floor exercise for the pectoral muscles, which underlie the breasts, is press-ups. A fit young person who is not overweight will probably be able to perform ten press-ups in rapid succession without the slightest difficulty. A tall person will have a lot more difficulty than a short person because of the extra leverage needed, so if you are very tall and find press-ups hard, don't worry.

But an older person or somebody who is overweight or otherwise unfit will experience difficulty since this exercise involves lifting all of the body weight on one's arms. A lighter variant of the same exercise is to grip a horizontal support, such as a solid window-sill, a horizontal bar, the arms of a large solid chair, etc so you exercise from an angle of roughly 45° instead of flat on the floor. Another way round this difficulty is to use light dumb-bell or other weights, lie flat on your back on the carpet and lift the weights twenty times from breast level to outstretched arms upwards.

Thighs and buttocks toners

These exercises are all a little heavier than the bust and waist exercises since they have to tone and stretch the large muscles involved in weight-bearing. Note that a cycling machine exercises very similar muscle groups and offers a simple alternative.

Thighs and buttocks 1

Find a relaxed stance with your feet comfortably apart and toes pointing as far sideways as is comfortable, hands on hips, then squat down on the rhythm of one-and-two and rise back to the start position on that same rhythm of one-and-two. At first you need only perform six of these over approximately half a minute but as your fitness increases, you can increase this to twelve.

Thighs and buttocks 2

Sit on the floor with your legs straight out in front of you, lean back onto your elbows and forearms until you find a comfortable position. Then, draw your knees up to your chest. Only now do you perform the exercise to that same one-and-two rhythm, stretching first your right leg to maximum with toe pointed outwards, alternating one-and-two from one leg to the other. Start with ten stretches for each leg and later increase to twenty.

Thighs and buttocks 3

Kneel on all fours, with your hands supporting your upper body. Then, to that same rhythm, first lift your right leg with knee bent to 90 degrees, then rest for a one-and-two on all fours before repeating with the other leg. Start with five exercises with either leg before building up to ten each leg.

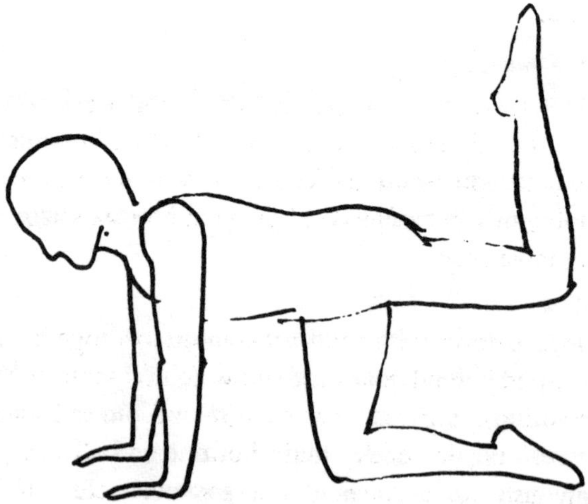

Thighs and buttocks 4

"Pretend cycling". Sit on the floor, then support your weight with your hands behind your back so you can lean back comfortably, lift your legs off the floor and to the one-and two rhythm, "cycle in air" with them. Exercise in this way for one to two minutes.

Step exercises

These are another form of aerobic exercise, based upon stepping up and down from a "bench". They are a good way to tone up buttocks and thighs and the exercises are very simple and easy to remember. You can save yourself a lot of money by making your own "bench", which amounts to a simple platform to step onto, from cheap board and covering it with a spare piece of carpet. Measure the width and depth of one of your stairs to give you an idea of the ideal size and height for you.

There are video routines to go with these or alternatively, if you prefer company, you could enrol in your local health club/sports centre for a class.

Spine exercises

Spine 1

Stand with feet comfortably apart and well balanced, lift both hands straight above your head. Then, to the one-and-two rhythm, arch your spine backwards. If you are a little unsteady when doing this, get a friend to hold your hips steady or lean back against a table edge.

Spine 2

Lie face down with your feet comfortably together and your hands clasped behind your head. Now, to that same one-and-two rhythm and keeping your legs straight and pressed together, lift both your upper body and both legs off the ground simultaneously for a count of one-and-two, return to base for another one-and-two, then repeat ten times.

CHAPTER SIX

Lifestyles

Alcohol

Alcohol is fine in moderation and provided you avoid driving. For many people it is part of our social culture and enjoyment. Here is a general guide:

Men should not drink more than two or three pints of beer three times a week. Women should not drink more than two pints or the equivalent three times a week. In some people who already have liver disease, alcohol is absolutely forbidden.

Alcohol equivalents: It will surprise many people to discover that a single whisky contains about the same amount of alcohol as half a pint of beer, a small sherry or a glass of wine.

Stress – the hidden menace

We know when we are under stress because we *feel* out of sorts. Some will fall victim to anxiety or bad nerves and suffer from dry mouth, jittery legs, difficulty sleeping, difficulties with concentration. While this may be common on rare occasions – for instance just before a driving test – if it describes you for long periods of time then there is no question that stress has gone way beyond what might be accepted as normal. Other giveaway symptoms are tension headache and flying off the handle at little upsets. A simple rule of thumb to determine if you are under excess stress or not is to ask your spouse or a very close relative or friend. They can often see the signs more clearly than you can. Perhaps even more common than the above symptoms of anxiety, other common presentations of stress include bowel gripes, abdominal bloating, muscles aching and tired most of the time, especially building up over those long hours of stressful employment.

Avoiding stress

I have used the term "avoiding" for good reason. In the majority of cases of prolonged stress, simple common sense will suggest a solution. If the stress is associated with work or the home, you can hardly avoid the occasion of the stress, but what you can do a great deal about is your reaction to that occasion. Here I would suggest that you just sit back a minute or two and analyse those situations which you find get you most "wound up". It is an excellent idea to get help from your spouse or best friend. Now list those situations on a sheet of paper. In a matter only of minutes you should have the causes of stress in your case on the sheet of paper in front of you.

Now ask yourself if you can possibly avoid such a situation. If yes is the answer, then do your best to avoid it. If, as I suspect will often be the case, no is the answer, look at the problem with an entirely different perspective.

Say to yourself: usually this winds me up but I am not going to allow it to do so. Take a deep breath, place the cause clearly in your mental sights, then take a mental step backwards from it and reduce its importance to you. These things can usually be put into a completely different perspective – in other words not seen as a vital problem that should have been solved five minutes ago but a trivial matter that is not going to be allowed to shorten your life. Think of the reaction of your work colleagues or even more perhaps of your family when in the face of such pressure you simply smile.

Other practical techniques that might help include the deliberate creation of time during the day to relax, for instance with light refreshment or even better, light exercise. For many people the opportunity for light exercise will take them completely away from the persistent nagging stress and it will also help reduce weight and keep the blood fats down as well.